10|14

D1379585

STRANDED!
Testing the Limits of Survival

Lost on a MOUNTAIN

by Meish Goldish

Consultant: Alex Van Steen, Mountain Guide
Rainier Mountaineering, Inc.
Ashford, Washington

BEARPORT
PUBLISHING

New York, New York

Credits

Cover, © Sergiy Zavgorodny/Shutterstock, © Scott E Read/Shutterstock, © Richard A McMillin/Shutterstock, and © Arsgera/Shutterstock; 4, © Arsgera/Shutterstock; 5, © Brian Dickinson; 6, © Brian Dickinson; 7, © Brian Dickinson; 8, © Christophe Boisvieux/Hemis/Alamy; 9, © Brian Dickinson; 11, © Karamysh/Shutterstock; 12, © Dennis Donohue /Shutterstock; 12M, © Patrick Poendl/Shutterstock; 13, © Nowak Lukasz/Shutterstock; 14–15, © Tibor Bognar/Alamy; 15, © Donna Cooper; 16–17, © Donna Cooper; 16MR, © g215/Shutterstock; 17, © Donna Cooper; 18, © Kastianz/Shutterstock; 19, © Latin Content/Getty; 20–21, © Keystone–France/Getty; 22, © Topham; 23ML, © Rolls Press/Popperfoto/Getty; 23BR, © Jon Freeman/Rex Features; 24, © Nevada Magazine; 25, © E+/Getty; 26, © Lucia Gonzalez; 27, © NBC/Getty; 28, © Alex Kosev/Shutterstock; 29, © Gorilla Images/Shutterstock.

Publisher: Kenn Goin
Editor: Jessica Rudolph
Creative Director: Spencer Brinker
Photo Research: Brown Bear Books Ltd

Library of Congress Cataloging-in-Publication Data

Goldish, Meish, author.
  Lost on a mountain / by Meish Goldish.
     pages cm.—(Stranded!: testing the limits of survival)
  Includes bibliographical references and index.
  ISBN-13: 978-1-62724-292-9 (library binding)
  ISBN-10: 1-62724-292-9 (library binding)
 1. Mountaineering—Juvenile literature. 2. Mountaineering accidents—Juvenile literature. 3. Survival—Juvenile literature. I. Title.
  GV200.23.C35G65 2015
  796.522--dc23
                                    2014017382

For more information, write to Bearport Publishing Company, Inc., 45 West 21st Street, Suite 3B, New York, New York 10010. Printed in the United States of America.

10 9 8 7 6 5 4 3 2 1

Contents

Alone at the Top

It was 2:30 A.M. on May 15, 2011. The temperature was below zero. Brian Dickinson struggled to climb up Mount Everest—the world's tallest mountain. He was just 1,000 feet (305 m) from the top, but the steep **slope** was covered in snow and ice. Brian inched his way up the mountain's "death zone." One wrong step could cause him to slip, fall, and possibly die.

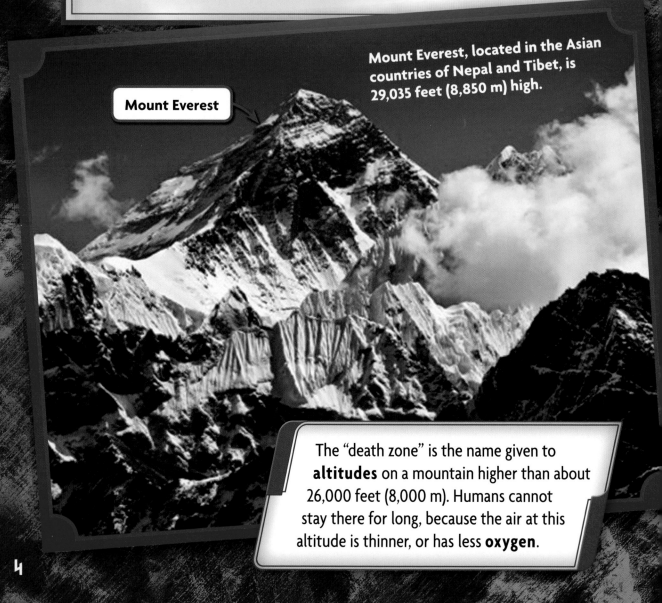

Mount Everest

Mount Everest, located in the Asian countries of Nepal and Tibet, is 29,035 feet (8,850 m) high.

The "death zone" is the name given to **altitudes** on a mountain higher than about 26,000 feet (8,000 m). Humans cannot stay there for long, because the air at this altitude is thinner, or has less **oxygen**.

Four hours later, Brian finally reached the **summit**. He thought, "Wow, I'm the highest person in the world right now." However, Brian's joy soon ended. Bright sunlight pierced through a crack in his sunglasses. The powerful rays burned his eyes. Alone and barely able to see, Brian would have to find his way down the icy mountain.

Brian stands on Mount Everest in 2011. He had to reach the top alone when his two climbing partners became ill and stayed at a camp lower on the mountain.

"Don't Panic"

Brian tried to stay calm. "Don't panic," he told himself. "If you panic, you die for sure." Squinting his eyes, he was able to see blurry shapes. He felt around and located the **fixed line** that ran along the mountainside. He held the rope tightly as he began to slowly make his way down the slope.

Brian had to walk along narrow ladders during part of his Mount Everest climb. Ropes, or fixed lines, and ladders have been placed on Everest by climbers to help others safely get around the mountain.

Suddenly, a terrible thought occurred to Brian. The tank of oxygen he was carrying held enough air to last only six more hours. His climbing partner had stored another tank farther down the mountain. Would Brian be able to reach it before running out of oxygen? With blurry eyesight, would he even be able to find the tank?

Brian wore an oxygen mask and oxygen tank in order to breathe while high on the mountain.

The air in Everest's death zone contains only one-third as much oxygen as the air at **sea level**. This is why climbers use oxygen tanks at very high altitudes.

A Rough Trip Down

While Brian climbed down, another emergency arose. He heard the mountain rumble and felt it shake. An **avalanche** had started! The downpour of heavy snow could have buried Brian alive, but he clung tightly to the fixed line as the snow rushed past him. Luckily, Brian was not harmed and he continued his journey.

An avalanche moves powerfully—like a train—down a mountainside. During an avalanche, a person can get buried und snow and die from a lack of oxygen.

A few hours later, though, Brian's oxygen tank was almost empty. He managed to find the new tank stored on the mountainside, but when he opened the air **valve**, nothing came out! Struggling for breath, he opened the valve again and again. On the third try, air rushed out! Now breathing normally, Brian was able to complete his trip down Everest.

From start to finish, Brian's climb up and down Everest took about 35 hours. Several weeks after the climb, his eyesight returned to normal.

At the bottom of Mount Everest, Brian (third from right) met up with friends who had waited for him to return.

What Is a Mountain?

Mount Everest, which Brian Dickinson risked his life to climb, is one of many mountains found around the world. A mountain is a tall **landform** that can rise thousands of feet above the ground.

Major Mountains of the World

Arctic Ocean

ASIA

NORTH AMERICA

Alps

EUROPE

Atlas Mountains

Himalaya Mountains

Mt. Everest

Rocky Mountains

Pacific Ocean

Atlantic Ocean

AFRICA

Pacific Ocean

SOUTH AMERICA

East Africa Mountains

Indian Ocean

Great Dividing Range

AUSTRALIA

Andes Mountains

N
W   E
S

◼ Mountain ranges

Southern Ocean

ANTARCTICA

Some mountains, such as Mount Everest and the Rocky Mountains, are in snowy, cold locations. Other mountains are in warm or hot areas. No matter what the surrounding **climate** is, mountain conditions get more **extreme** the higher a person climbs. The thinner air makes breathing more difficult. At around 8,000 feet (2,438 m), thin air can cause people to have headaches and **nausea**. Much higher up, the lack of oxygen can be deadly.

Rocky Mountains

A group of mountains is called a range. The Rocky Mountains are the largest mountain range in North America.

Mountain Life

Although conditions high on a mountain can be extreme, some plants and animals have found ways to survive. The plants grow close to the ground, so they are protected from strong winds. Some animals, such as yaks, have long, thick hair that keeps them warm in very cold temperatures. Snow leopards have large paws and long tails to help them keep their balance as they hunt on steep, rocky slopes.

Many mountain plants grow in the cracks of rocks. This gives the plants added protection from high winds.

Snow leopards live in the mountains of Asia. They can jump as far as 50 feet (15.24 m) from one steep rock to another.

Few people live at very high, cold altitudes. However, in Nepal, the Sherpas are a **tribe** of people who have lived in the mountains for hundreds of years. Many Sherpas serve as **guides** to mountain climbers who come to Mount Everest.

Sherpas raise animals and grow crops that can survive in the cold weather. They often use yaks to carry supplies, such as tents and food.

A Dangerous Drive

A mountain in a hot climate can be just as dangerous as a mountain in a cold climate. In July 2010, Donna Cooper drove with her daughter, Gina, and a friend, Jenny Leung, into Death Valley National Park. As the group crossed the desert, a wrong turn led them into the park's mountains.

Death Valley National Park stretches from California to Nevada. It is the hottest and driest national park in the United States. The park includes both deserts and mountains.

The temperature was 125°F (52°C) in the mountains. The women became hot and thirsty as they kept driving—searching for a way out. By nightfall, the car was almost out of gas. Despite the terrible heat, the women slept in the car with the windows rolled up in case mountain lions or bears came near. When the car wouldn't start the next morning, the women used stones to write HELP in giant letters on the ground. Would a pilot flying overhead notice the sign?

Dust on the Coopers' car gave them

Signaling For Help

Later that day, the three women spotted an airplane in the sky. Gina flashed a **compact disc** (CD) at the sun, hoping the **reflection** of light would catch the pilot's attention. Jenny waved a yellow blanket. Unfortunately, the pilot saw neither signal.

The woman began to think it could be a long time before rescuers found them. Their water bottles were empty, so they decided to chew on pine needles. Donna knew the leaves contained some **moisture** and **nutrients**.

At one point when the group was lost, Jenny (below) walked to try to find help.

Pine needles are the leaves of a pine tree. They get their name from their needle shape. The leaves contain vitamin C and are often used to make tea.

After chewing on the needles, the women tried desperately to start the car again. This time it worked! Amazingly, the three managed to find their way off the mountain. They remained lost in the desert but were saved the next day when rescue workers spotted them from a helicopter. Although the women had been worried, Donna said, "Never for a second did I doubt that we would make it out of there."

Gina (left), Donna (center), and Jenny (right) were thrilled when a helicoper rescue team found them.

A Deadly Crash

The women in Death Valley survived partly by chewing on mountain plants. Yet what can people do when there is nothing at all to eat? This is what happened in October 1972, when an airplane with 45 people on board crashed into the snowy, freezing Andes Mountains. Eighteen people were killed during the crash.

This photo shows a portion of the Andes Mountains, between Argentina and Chile, near the spot where the plane crashed.

The Andes, in South America, is the world's longest mountain range. It stretches about 4,300 miles (6,920 km).

The survivors took shelter in the plane's broken **fuselage**, waiting to be rescued. At night, the temperature dropped to a deadly -30°F (-34°C). Ten days passed, but no help came. The survivors had eaten all the food from the plane, and there were no plants or animals in the mountains that they could eat. The starving passengers faced an emergency: What would they eat now?

Survivors rested outside the plane when the temperature was warm enough.

From Bad to Worse

Inside the fuselage, the hungry survivors held a meeting. They decided to eat the flesh of the dead passengers whose frozen bodies were **preserved** in the snow. Roberto Canessa, a survivor, admitted it was a "disgusting decision" to eat **corpses**. However, he said he desperately wanted to live to see his mother again.

The following week, things grew even worse for the survivors. One afternoon, an avalanche roared down the mountainside. Giant piles of snow crashed against the fuselage. Eight people were killed. Those who survived were trapped inside the plane. It took them two days to dig free from the piles of snow.

EREA URUG

During the avalanche, three of the survivors were badly hurt. In the next few weeks, they died as a result of their injuries.

A corpse (above) lies frozen in the snow next to the fuselage.

One Last Hope

The people who were still alive had survived a plane crash and an avalanche, but they had little hope for a rescue. On a radio that was saved from the plane crash, they heard news reports that the search for the missing plane had been called off after attempts to find it failed. Two survivors, Nando Parrado and Roberto Canessa, decided that their only hope was to hike across the snowy Andes Mountains to seek help.

Roberto Canessa in 1972

The two men attached seat cushions from the plane to their shoes so they could walk on the snow without sinking. After walking for ten days, Nando and Roberto finally found a ranch worker, who notified Chilean government authorities. Seventy-two days after the plane crash, helicopters came to rescue the surviving passengers.

Crash survivors wave to the helicopters coming to rescue them.

Only 16 of the 45 passengers survived being stranded in the Andes for 72 days.

In 2002, Roberto Canessa (center) and two other survivors visited the crash site.

Trapped Upside Down

The Andes survivors were saved because two passengers tried to find help. However, at times it may be best to stay put. In December 2013, a family of six drove into the Seven Troughs Range in Nevada to spend the day playing in the snow. Suddenly, their car ran off a dirt road, rolled down the mountain slope, and landed upside down.

Seven Troughs Range

Amazingly, nobody was hurt. However, with no help nearby and poor cell phone service, the family was stranded inside the car. Outside, the temperature was a deadly -21°F (-29°C). James Glanton, the father, knew that his family had to stay warm to avoid frostbite—or even worse, freezing to death. Yet without heat or blankets, how could they survive?

Body parts that are affected by frostbite can turn black.

Frostbite is caused by **exposure** to extreme cold and high winds. In even a short amount of time, some areas of the body can freeze. In the worst cases, frozen body parts, such as fingers or toes, need to be **amputated**.

"All the Right Decisions"

James came up with an idea. He put the car's spare tire outside in the snow and placed rocks in the tire's hole. Then he set the tire on fire to heat up the rocks. Finally, he brought the rocks inside the car to warm the air.

The family's car, upside down, on the mountain

When news spread that the family was missing, around 200 people helped search for them. Luckily, weak signals from James's cell phone led rescuers to the right area. After two days, the family was found in good condition. Survival expert Joseph Teti said they had made "all the right decisions" by not going out in the deadly cold. The family's experience proved once again that people lost on a mountain can survive by making wise choices.

Paul Burke, a rescue team leader, said of James Glanton's rock-heating plan, "I have never heard of such a thing, but I think it was pretty clever of him."

After being rescued, James and his family were interviewed on television. They talked about how they survived being stranded on a mountain.

Mountain Survival Tips

If you plan to visit a mountain, follow these tips to help you survive.

- ✔ Wear or pack proper clothing for cold or hot mountain weather, such as hats, coats, gloves, and boots.
- ✔ Pack the necessary mountain gear, such as sunglasses, a compass, a map, sunscreen, a flashlight, and a first-aid kit.
- ✔ Bring bottled water and canned or dried food.
- ✔ Pack a cell phone with plenty of spare batteries.

Supplies for a mountain trip may include things such as water, food, a flashlight, and a first-aid kit.

- ✔ Tell people where you're going, so they'll know where to look if you get lost.
- ✔ Bring matches or lighters to start a fire in case you need to stay warm or alert people that you're stranded.
- ✔ If you get lost on a mountain, stay in an open area and wear bright clothing, so a rescue plane or helicopter pilot can see you easily. Make a large signal on the ground, such as three piles of leaves or rocks arranged in a triangle.
- ✔ Build a small shelter that will protect you from rain, wind, snow, and insects as you sleep.
- ✔ Stay calm and make a plan. Think carefully about what you need to do to survive until help arrives.

People who hike in the mountains should wear the proper gear, such as gloves and boots.

Glossary

altitudes (AL-ti-toodz) heights above sea level

amputated (AM-pyoo-*tay*-tid) cut off from the body because of an injury or infection

avalanche (AV-uh-lanch) a giant amount of snow, ice, or rock that slides down a mountain slope with great force

climate (KLYE-mit) the usual weather in a place

compact disc (KOM-pakt DISK) a round, shiny piece of plastic used for recording music, videos, or other computer information

corpses (KORPS-iz) dead bodies

exposure (ek-SPOH-zhur) being left uncovered and without protection against something, such as extreme cold or heat

extreme (ek-STREEM) very great or severe

fixed line (FIHKST LINE) a rope attached to a mountainside that mountain climbers hold as they move up or down the slope

fuselage (FYOO-suh-lahzh) the main body of an aircraft where passengers, crew, and cargo are carried

guides (GIDEZ) people or animals that lead or show the way to others

landform (LAND-form) a natural feature on Earth's surface

moisture (MOIS-chur) small particles of water or other liquid

nausea (NAW-zhuh) a sick feeling in one's stomach

nutrients (NOO-tree-uhnts) proteins, vitamins, fats, and other things that are needed by people and animals to stay healthy

oxygen (OK-suh-juhn) a colorless, odorless gas that is found in the air and water, and that animals and people need to breathe to survive

preserved (pri-ZURVD) protected and kept in the original condition

reflection (ri-FLEK-shuhn) the bouncing of light rays off a shiny surface

sea level (SEE LEV-*uhl*) the average height of the surface of the ocean

slope (SLOHP) ground that slants downward or upward

summit (SUHM-it) the very top of a mountain

tribe (TRIBE) a group made up of many families that share the same language and customs

valve (VALV) a movable part that controls the flow of a liquid or gas through a pipe or other passageway

Bibliography

Bronski, Peter. *At the Mercy of the Mountains: True Stories of Survival and Tragedy in New York's Adirondacks.* Guilford, CT: Lyons (2008).

Dickinson, Brian. *Blind Descent: Surviving Alone and Blind on Mount Everest.* Carol Stream, IL: Tyndale House (2014).

Kuhne, Cecil, ed. *Near Death in the Mountains: True Stories of Disaster and Survival (Vintage Departures).* New York: Vintage (2008).

Parrado, Nando, and Vince Rause. *Miracle in the Andes: 72 Days on the Mountain and My Long Trek Home.* New York: Crown (2006).

Read More

Galko, Francine. *Mountain Animals (Animals in Their Habitats).* Chicago: Heinemann (2003).

Jenkins, Steve. *The Top of the World: Climbing Mount Everest.* Boston: Houghton Mifflin (1999).

Sandler, Michael. *Mountains: Surviving on Mt. Everest (X-treme Places).* New York: Bearport (2006).

Learn More Online

To learn more about surviving on a mountain, visit
www.bearportpublishing.com/Stranded!

Index

About the Author

*Meish Goldish has written more than 200 books for children.
His book* Disabled Dogs *was a Junior Library Guild Selection in 2013.
He lives in Brooklyn, New York, and likes to visit the Catskill Mountains.*